D0921777

EVEREST:

the
Ultimate
Hump.

written & illustrated by T. Knight

Menasha Ridge Press
Birmingham, Alabama

EVEREST · The Ultimate Hump
©1999 Tami Knight
Cover art © Grant Tatum & T. Knight
cover photo © Alpine ASCENT
        International collection 1992
PUBLISHED Menasha Ridge Press
           700 S. 28th St # 206
           Birmingham , AL , 35233
           1 - 800· 247 · 9437
           www. menasharidge .com

FIRST EDITION FIRST PRINTING
All rights reserved
CIP
Knight , Tami , 1959·
     Everest : The Ultimate Hump/
     written & illustrated by T. Knight
        p· cm.
ISBN 0 · 89732 · 392 · 5
     1. Everest , Mount (China and Nepal
        -- caricatures and cartoons)
     2. Mountaineering -- caricatures
        and cartoons
     3. American wit and humour -
        pictoral
     I . Title

NC1429 . K586A4 1999

741 . 5973 -- dc21 99 - 33429
            CIP

Dedicated to those 3 who
suffer me the most... my husband
Bini LeBlanc & our 2 thugs
Isaac & Dominique
But it's also for these crazy people:
David Dornian, Jill Haras, Mike
Jones, Geoff Powter, David S Roberts,
Chic Scott & Steve Threndyle.

BeeCuzzz it's There! YES! YES! YES! That's why! It Haz NUTHIN' to do with EGO nuthin' NUTHIN' nuthin'! IT'S CUZ IT'S THERE

yes indeedie-doo!

EVEREST
The Ultimate Hump...
CONTAINZ....

Chapter ONE

More

MORE

MORE

GOOFY

WAYS & REASONS TO CLIMB EVEREST

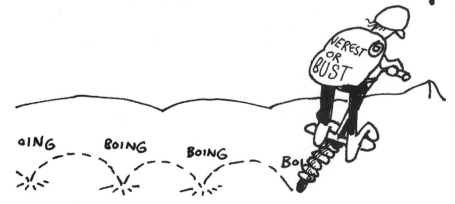

I'm planning the waterbirth for the South Col and then I shall summit the following day with my newborn.
IT's my First Baby
I'm SO HAPPY
I KNOW EXACTLY WHUT I AM DOING
Why yes I am having it FILMED.
©Knight

I am a poet
So is my dog
I have changed my name to Summi Twut Ever
And my dog's to Oneverest.
We will Summit Mt. Everest & then write many poems about it.
We will publish them ourselves in a very very thick book
©T.Knight

I'm gonna climb Mt. Everest wearin a Hamster suit so EVERYONE WILL BE
NICE to ANIMALS
the
Nice
I ♥ ANIMALS
GORE
HAVE YOU HUGG YOUR HAMST

THE DIANAS ON EVEREST EXPEDITION ARGUE ABOUT WHAT TO CALL THEIR FORTHCOMING BOOK.....

Birds & FISH are dyin'...
This is bad
I shall CLIMB EVEREST & tell the WHOLE WORLD that BIRDS & FISH are DYING.
EVEREST
BIRDS & FISH
Gotta stop dyinG
EXPEDISHIN
©J. Knight

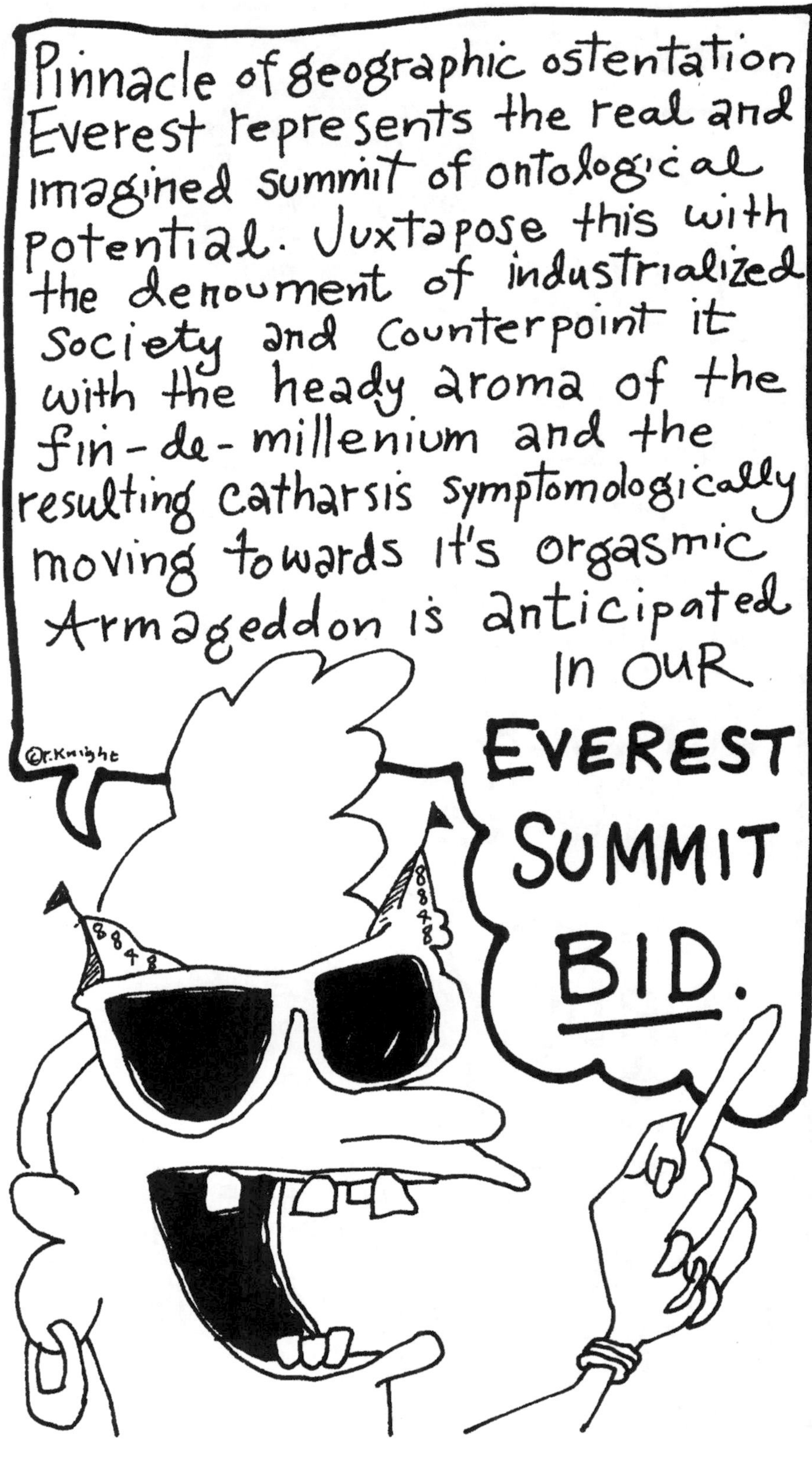
Pinnacle of geographic ostentation Everest represents the real and imagined summit of ontological potential. Juxtapose this with the denoument of industrialized society and counterpoint it with the heady aroma of the fin-de-millenium and the resulting catharsis symptomologically moving towards it's orgasmic Armageddon is anticipated in OUR EVEREST SUMMIT BID.
©T. Knight
8848
8848

CHAPTER 2

THE ANCIENT ART OF FUNDING

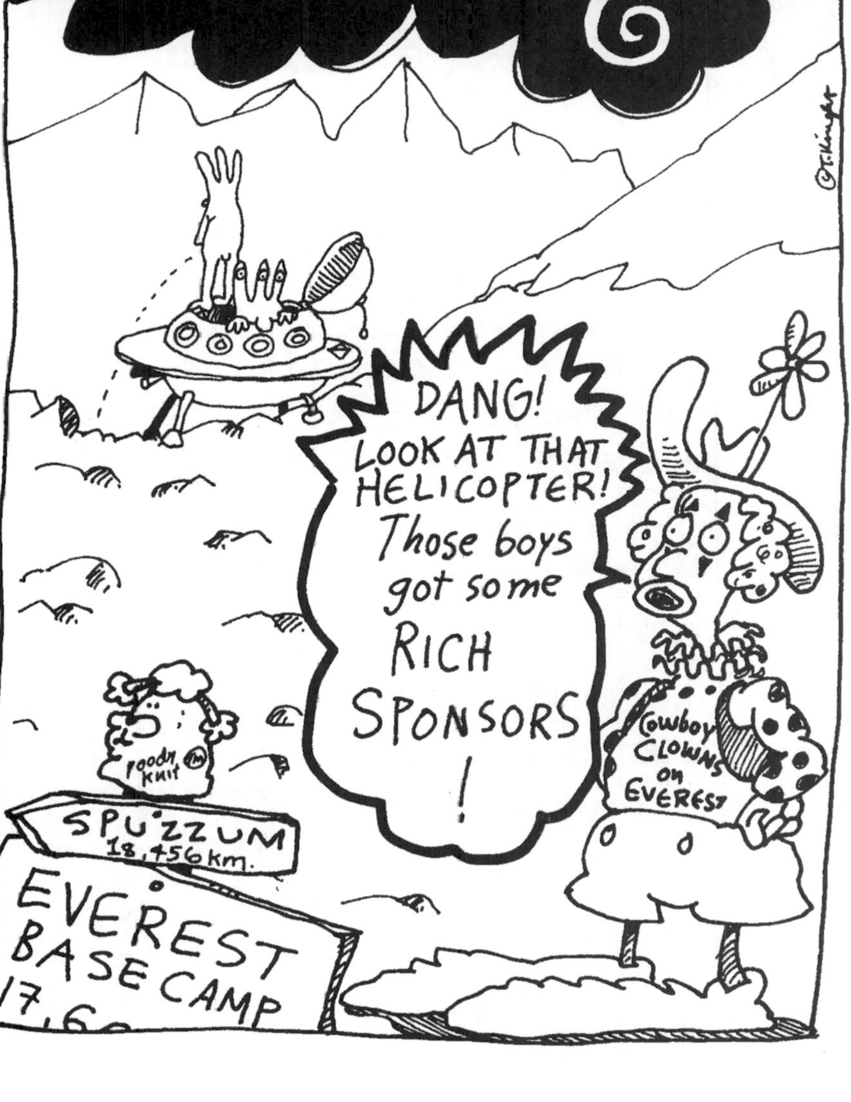

ANOTHER PRESENTATION

the EXPEDITION of INDECISION

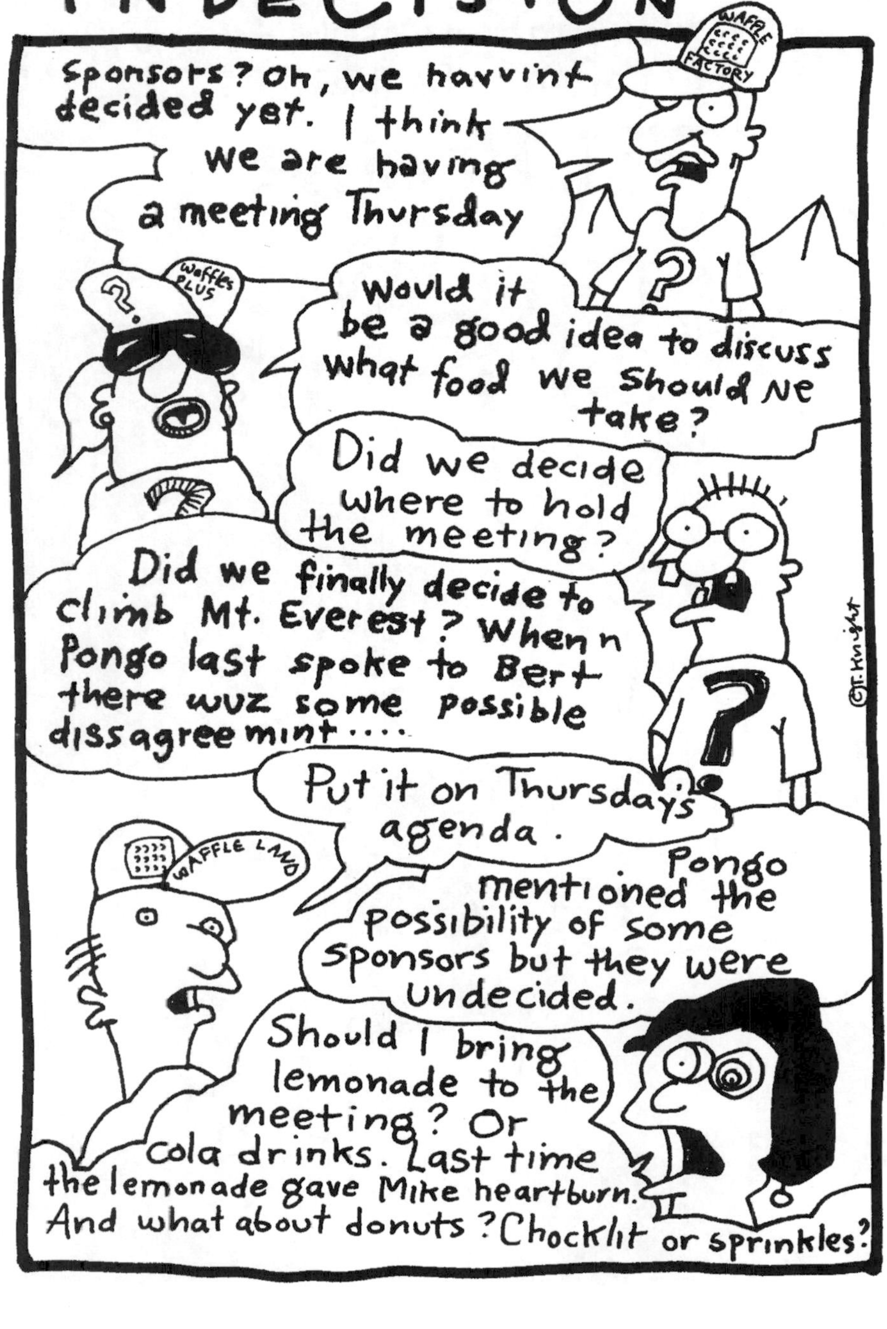

eanut
tter
I can
oxygen
our
sponsors
satelli
nood
ice
This pristine bea-
places populated
happily digging
otatoes in the
fields. Today we
the wea-
dear Mom
Fluzzy is th
so am I ho
He dobbled over
to puke wurse agai
is this all worth it
this huge big deep pain
I lift
from the desk of
Miriam LaRo
Gale force w
so glad we
espresso maker
Camp II I am
excited treasure
hunt; Rolfo is so
gorgeous I luv
his tight butt
dear d
toda
loads t
ridge t
heavy

So how about I be Harvey ONE an' you Harvey TWO an' him...
That's a stupid idea
We can't use our last names. I got no clue in Hell how to pronounce "WYRTZ"
Simple. It rhymes with "Flyrtz"
...and arnt you Mr. Helpful
EXCUSE ME ... but I'm with the EXPEDITION OF INDECISION! I could help you not decide about what you are undecided about.
Qué?
WAIT A SEC!
COULD THIS BE?
I FEEL WEIRD
I MIGHT HAVE JUST MADE A DECISION!
Three hats?
I couldn't decide..
Harv Everest
Harv Everest
Expedition of Indecision sponsored by ?
TWO Heads everest expedition
10/6
©J. Knight

ALTITUDE ABOVE 26,169.23'
IS KNOWN TO CLIMBERS AS
THE DEATH ZONE
WITHOUT SUPPLEMENTAL OXYGEN,
THE BRAINS OF NORMAL PEOPLE
SHRIVEL UP AND DIE....

I must be dying
there'z not one p·p-princess Diana there'z six
Oh look one of those awful papparazzi
How can we help you?
Better 'n' CHICKEN GIZZERDS
RedWIGGLER FISHIN BAIT
CHIX 'n' Fellerz
platinum sponger
FISHIN red Wiggler BAIT
©T.Knight

THE ... HAMSTER-PERSON ... IS .... DEAD ... HAND ME ... ... THE .. KNIFE !!!
WHOOO
Whee
I ♥ Animals
GORE
BE NICE to ANIMA
Mt Everest Expediti

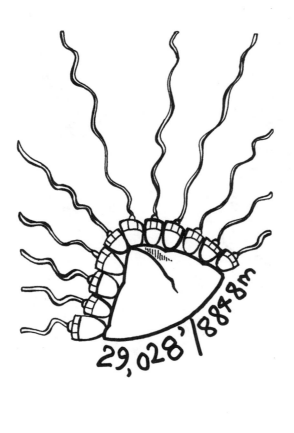

29,028' / 8848m

chapter 4

CYBERHUMP
EVEREST
29.029

the WEBSITE

CLICK yer BLISS
& SCROLL freely

VIRTUALLY CLIMB to the
VIRTUAL highest point of
the known VIRTUAL WURLD
Be a VIRTUAL Hero !!!

BOLSTER YER SAGGING CAREER by SUMMITTING

click here fer opportoonities in **FAME**

click here fer oppertunities in **FORTUNE**

click here fer opportunyties in **HAPPINESS**

LINKS to MORE ★ $ ♥

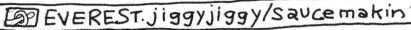

EVEREST.jiggyjiggy/saucemakin'

EVEREST

PORN

YOU MUST BE 18 YEARS OF AGE OR OLDER TO VISIT THIS SITE. YOU MAY NEED TO VERIFY YOUR AGE. BE PREPARED TO ENTER YOUR MOM'S PHONE NUMBER FOR AGE VERIFICATION.

 EXIT

 Free Preview

 Members ONLY

Click  Heer

THIS Inflatable sheep DOUBLES as a PORTABLE HYPERBARIC UNIT.

click  heer

XXXX EVEREST HEROS IN THEIR UNWASHED UNDERWEAR.

click  Here

TIPS to SPANKIN' the MONKEY ABOVE 8000 m.

©T.Knight

WOW Reuul GROOVY

LIVE AUDIO from Mt. EVEREST

ultimatehump/clipclip/chopchop.spew

LISTEN TO THAT HUMP

the SOUND of FROZEN DIGITS amputated without ANAESTHETIC

An ULTIMATE HUMPSITE First the FIRST BOWLING BALL SWALLOWERS ON EVEREST SWALLOW THEIR BALLS!

the Marcel Marceau ONE HAND CLAPPING on EVEREST EXPEDITION

©T. Knight

EVEREST/nexttimeaskyermother/

Mt EVEREST FAQ'S

? IZ IT TRUE THERE'S NO OXYGEN UP THERE CUZ SO MANY PEOPLE HAVE GONE AN' BREATHED IT ALL UP ?

? CAN I TAKE MY DOG ?

? HOW DID THEY GIT THE redWIGGLER FISHIN' BAIT TO THE SUMMIT?

.... AND, WHY?

? IZ IT POSSIBLE TO GROW A THOUSAND POUND 'Atlantic Giant' PUMPKIN AT THE SOUTH COL?

? IF NOBODY IS THERE TO HEAR THE AVALANCHE ON THE MOUNTAIN, DOES IT MAKE ANY SOUND?

©T.Knight

POST YER OWN BLISS

HUMP THE PAGE OF FAME 'n' GLORY

"Acheevmint is the constant process of seein how far you can shove your head up your ass."
— Lester X Pinfester; leader; Head-Up-Ass Everest Expedition.

FOTO OF THE WEEK

29,028 people on the summit all at once. Recognize anyone ya know?

the ASSAULT EVEREST ATTACK CHALLENGE CONQUEST PROJECT.

ENTER OUR CONTEST

THE THREE STOOGES LOOKALIKES on EVEREST

WINNERS PICKED EV'RY DAY! woo woo woo

COOL CORPSES STILL UP THERE

CLICK & ZOOM IN ON YER FAVE

WHAT PART OF MALLORY IS THIS ???

Guess correctly
WIN A PRIZE
enter answer &

| I | ▼ | GO! |

COOL CORPSE FACTS

- They keep LONGER when FROZEN!
- Of the 25 bodies on the mountain, 19 are missin their boots!
- A corpse clad in NEON PINK GORETEX IS VISIBLE from the MIR Space Station!

 # CLICK HERE
fer a **Free Eulogy**

"I lift up mine eyes...."

"O, dang, yer dead..."

"Daddy why didnt ya have life insurance...."

EVEREST day 2 day DISPATCH...

MORNIN' RITUALS

Sun 6 May – Base Camp "I got out of my sleeping bag, put the kettle on and went to the potty. Ten people stood before me in the line." —Prunella "Perky Pru" Snitzly

OH, SO FUNNY

Tues 8 May – Advanced Base Camp – "Jeremy used Snerd's frisbee as a dish for his noodle dinner. Snerd was not happy with noodle chunkies on his favrit toy." – Binkly Farshnikkle

NEWS BULLETIN

Tues 8 May - Press Release from the Fancy Donuts on Everest Exp'n – "We got one dozen chocolate frosted and two dozen sprinkles donuts to the summit."

FOR REAL

Fri 11 May - Camp IV; South Col "I hereby report to you rocks at this altitude are yellowish brown to bluish grey in colour and snow beigy pink to pinkish beige with some yellow dis--coloration." - Prof. E. Duroid; Heavy Science on Everest Project.

chapter FIVE

Wake Up to EVEREST
THE COFFEE
WOW
IT'S, LIKE...
I'M "INTO THIN AIR"
Take me to THE CLIMB
©T. Knight

experience the vicarious thrill of BEIN' THERE & DOIN' THAT
BRUSH With EVEREST toothpaste™
Yes
brush
skrub
skrub
brush
brush
skrub
skrub
EVEREST toothpaste
©T. Knight

Everesti ❀ Doll

today's episode: I love the serac
                          doom doom doom

Cho and Mo dress warmly and head to the Icefall.

Lung shows Mah how to peform a tracheotomy with a pen knife

...but before we start the slides of our journey to the summit of Everest I'd like to thank our sponsors without whom weed never bin able to go: XQ Alpine Backpacks and travel luggage; Rumpyropes, manufactchering fine climbing ropes since 1994, SLIME-gel power xx-trem food; NoLEEK fabrics purveyers of high-kwality rugged fabrix fer outdoor recreational purposes; WARMYKINS sleeping bags, hi-loft lo-weight warmykins for all yer outdoor sleeping needs; N-SO-REST mats they're gonna keep yer buttski warm even on snow; LASE-IT shoelaces fer all yer lacing needs; SKWELCH buttplugs; KLEENLY PERF water filters take even viruses outta the water; SQWIRRL nuts and seeds; FLAME-O chili powders, curries, spice, hot peppers, nitroglycerine, and saltpeter, MeZHUR tape measures and other measuring supplies for all those measuring need; FOAMETTE Styrofoam cups, saucers, bowls, demitasses, bordeaux glasses, coffee cups LOOK FOR OUR NEW styreen cup specially designed for herbal teas; PICCY PIXPERFECT camerus and laserdevelopped wrapparound technologically advanced film; SNARFAMUNDO chains; WHALE ha___ ___ns for all yer harpooning needs; Redwiggler Fishin Bait the o___ ___er summit Mt. Everest; CHIMP'S FAVVY bananas mangoe___ ___ papayas; FLESHY cat products; FRANKS BEST savings ___ ___ and pawn shop, Chunky Dog pet foods; KO-MO-DO drago___ ___ducts; FLATTY's pancakes, waffles & crepe suzettes DON'T BE ___ ATTY EAT AT FLATTY's like they say on TV; did I mention ___ ___ plugs? Oh and what about those kind people who a___ ___atels to carry to the summit and how could I eve___ ___nderful generous supp___ ort of all the wonderful frien___ ___mily who lent their love & devotion I could never have m___ ___d ___ happen without their generous assistance and I have a ___cial ___ they sent us of P.S. 1089 and her lovely class ___ ___ th a___ ___ whole weeks money they saved by going wi___ ___lu___ ___my cat and an extra special hug to Dr. lex ___hk w___ ___ for the time I was on the mo___ nt___ n an ye___ ___ it it folks SO ON WITH THE SLIDESHOW!!!)

Zzz z z z zz z z
Zzz zzz zz zzz zzz zz z
Z Zzz zzzz z
Z z snooo zz
Z zz zz 7z

CHAPTER SIX

Everest, Texas

....you got it in the dang bag! Why I'm goin' myself! Got this fancy mountain climbin' kit & y'oughta see my guide. A right pretty thang!
Why.... R.T. Tailgator III, you couldn't git your sorry ass to th'top of a week-old armadilla turd.
The hell I can't, Buck Blackthorn.
©T.Knight
18
roll roll roll roll roll roll roll roll
plop

By the way, Ross... WHAR the Sam Hill is Mt. Evvyrest, ANYWAY?
Praps you left it in your Turbo Saab.
No no no son ... the mountain, Mt. Evyrest. Wher'z THAT dang mountain?
Why it's in the kingdom of Nepal.
?
South o' Chinese Tibet. On th' other side of the wurld!
WHAT! China? THET WUZZINT IN THE BROCHURE!
18
©T. Knight

Ross ... Soon az we're dun here, son, ah've a l'il errand fer yew t'run.
Yes sir!
Tailgator? Yew talk faster on that thing then ma ex wife.
Beep
18
©T. Knight

Boss!! I found somethin'!
EVEREST
EVEREST North Face box 296,355 more rocks
EVEREST West Ridge Box 965,322 Rocks Some snow
EVEREST Mallory Site Legal bullshit
EVEREST box 6,251,398 Khumbu Icefall ice + bones
EVEREST West Ridge Box 965,321 Rocks
EVEREST
EVEREST YellowSpur box 365,111 yellow rocks
EVEREST YellowSpur box 365,110 yellow snow
EVEREST West Ridge
poody knit
EVEREST Western cwm Sector ZQ79(i) Box 1,777,682 Snow ?? , O2 bottle
]]]

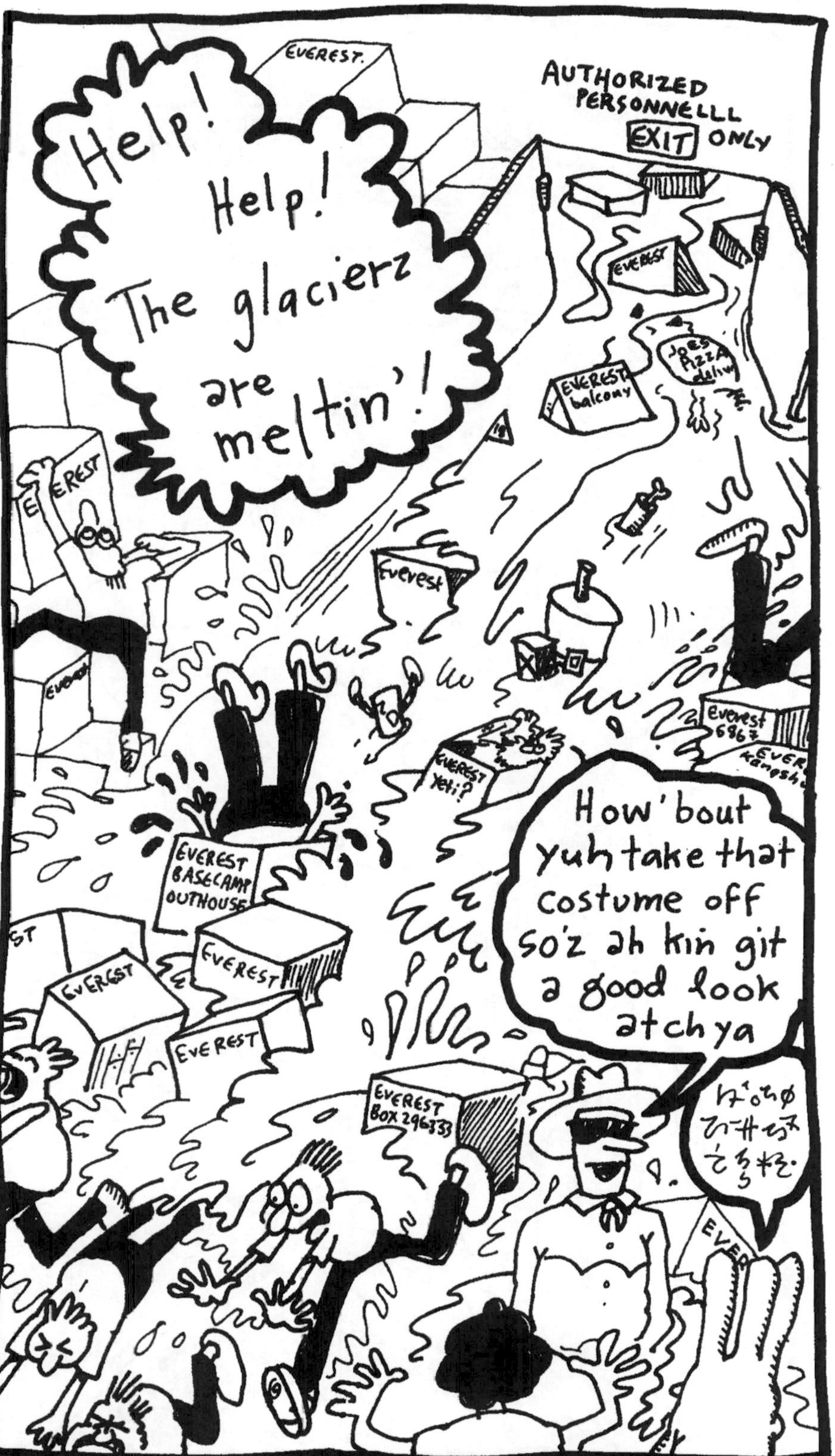

... an' Ross? you remember Who ol' Buck is front man fer...
Speak up son ah c'aint hear ya..
!!!!!
Whassat? Sea MONKEYS? Never heard o' them. But see if they got muscle enough an' hire 'em fer the project.

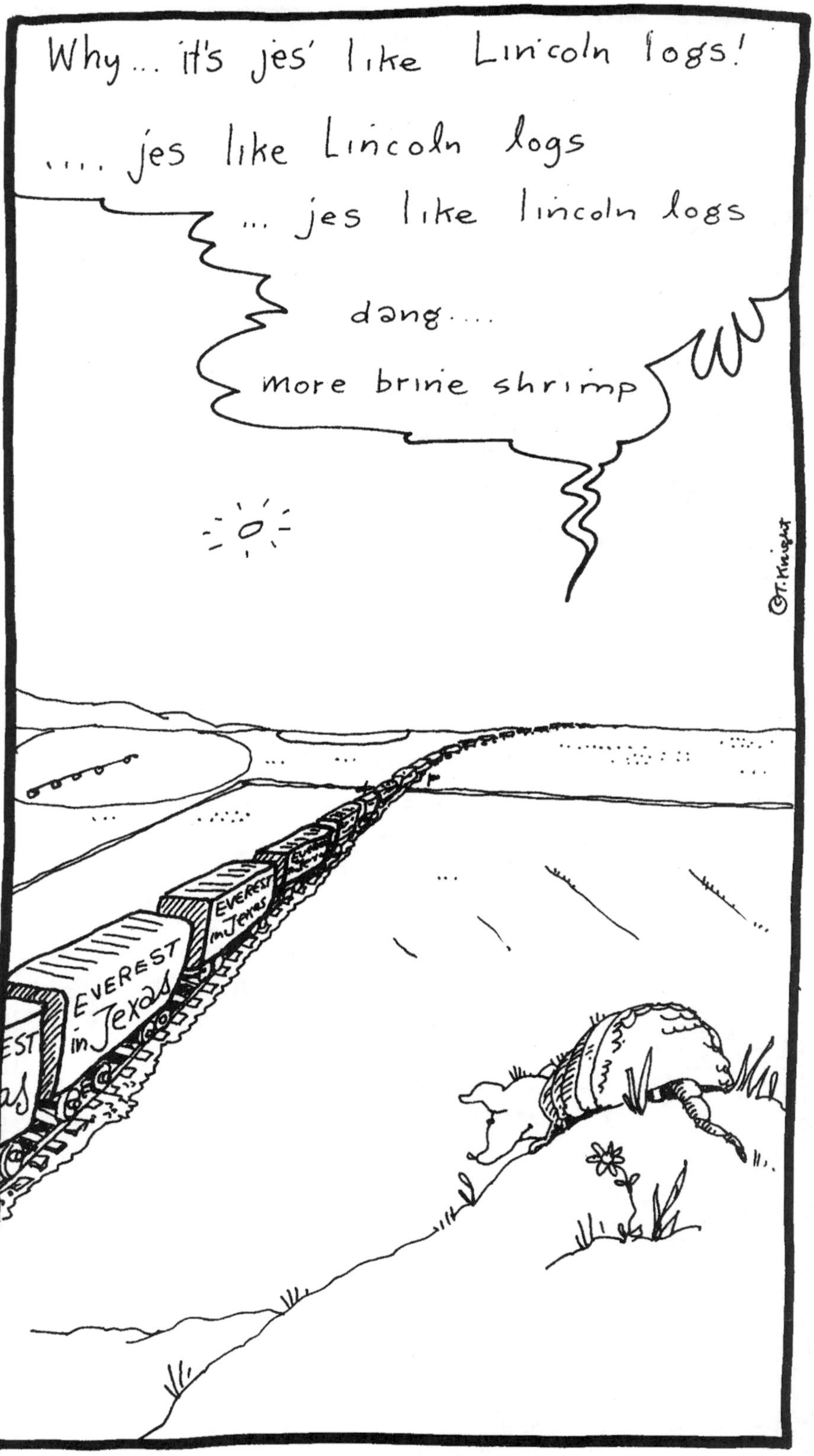

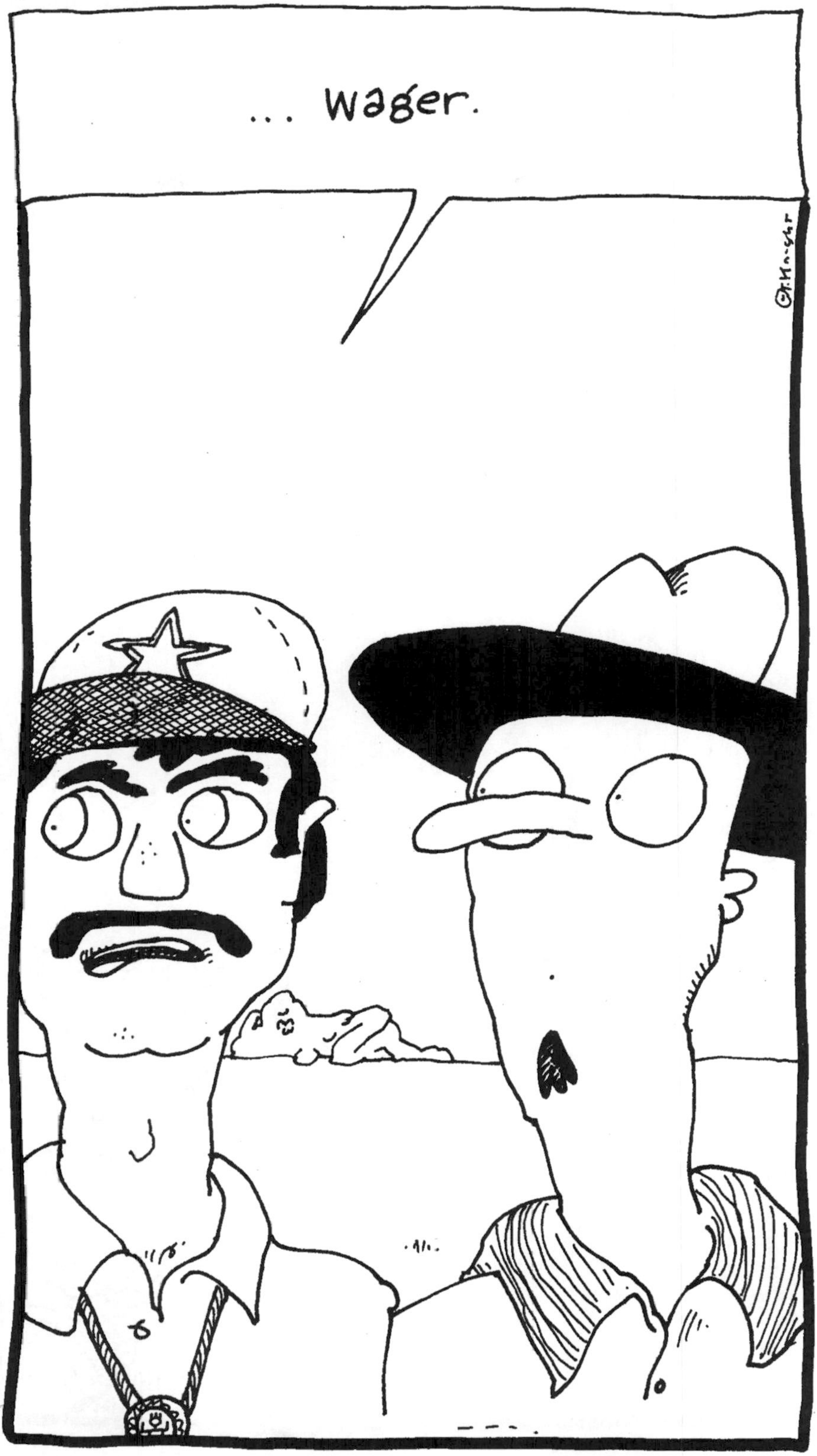
... wager.

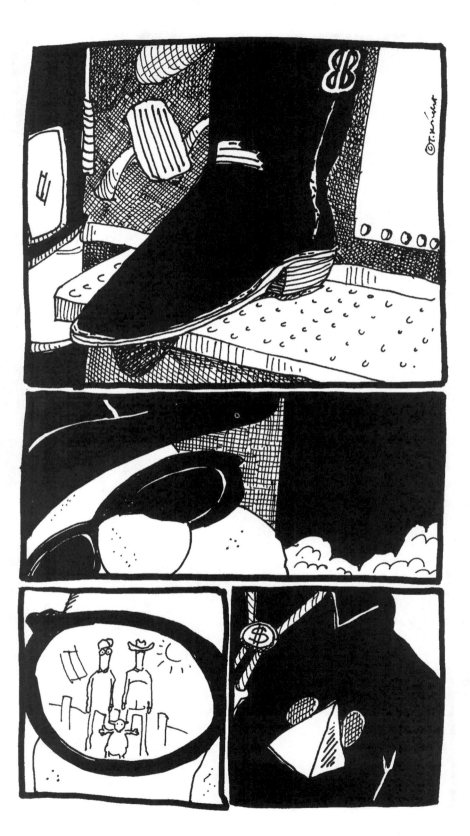

".... hand over that mountain."

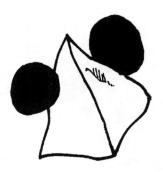

EVERESTLAND MINIGOLF

THE MOST POPULAR EVERESTLAND FOTO-OP SPOT

the MALLORY site

AAACKNOOLIDJMINTS!!!

Certainly I draw it as I see it but there's many many a time when folks stepped in to either offer a sug-gestion "THat's not very funny y'know" or to smack the back of my head with their version of a 400lb halibut.

First off I need to extend more then hugs, kisses, gratitude, etc to my husband Bini LeBlanc & our 2 thugs (commonly called 'children but we know better) Isaac, the 9½ yr old human tornado & his sister Dominique, 8, "I wanna dog, jus' like THAT."

I'd hereby like to congrachyoolate Bob Sehlinger @ Menasha Ridge Press fer retaining his sanity durin' this book's production... yeah, I KNOW more then half the costs were in phone bills between my home here in Canada & the offices in Alabama! Huzzah!

Ev'ry book needs an editor & mine is Editorius Extreemis (southeastern sub-species), the redoubtable & incomparable... Jaime's Dad!! His friends know him az Bnd. Zehmer thet iz Jennie calls him "husband" so back off all you droolin' wimmin

Poodyknit

Haw Haw Haw — Fer continuin' to publish my sorry ass in their fine rag, it's neccc-esssary fer me to grovel fer the likes of Onan Raleigh (publisher @ large), Alison Wonder Woman Osius, Dave the Pegg & who kin fergit Mike Kennedy.

Fer listenin' to my conflabulated psykobabble & smiling & nodding BUT NOT backin' away hugs 'n' kissis to Jill Haras, David Dornian, Mike Jones, Chic Scott, Gottfried PooPoo, Leslie DeMarsh, Josh Gardly Bee Blum-ental, Zac Bolan, Steve Threndyle, Woody, & David S Roberts.

Too LARGE! Too LARGE!

EVEREST Bowlin Ball Swallowerz

And not to forget these great people (o.k they might not all be completely "people") for various favours past, present & future... Ed Douglas, Verm, cb, Hat Naylor, Hannah Galloway, John Wason & the crazies @ Patagonia, Paul Malon, Jen Chow, Craig Luebben, William Nealy, Peter og Anne Croft, Wendy Croft, Hillary & Suzanne @ MOUNTAINFREAK, François LeBlanc, John 'SUPER REP' Campbell, Michel Guérin, the Beeck sisters, Fern Hietkamp, my brother Tony & Mum & Dad, Alan Formanek, John Burbidge, John Long, anitafrita, YC & Malinda Chouinard, Bubba B

"May the FARCE be with ewe"
xxo

$4.?
1.WOX

baaaaah

PIKA MOUNTAINEERIN' ® velcro mitts & Gumboots.

She found his corpse,
pants around his ankles,
the magazine spread open
to the Everest Centerfold